Past Work Future Work

Andrew Einspruch

Past Work, Future Work

Text: Andrew Einspruch
Design: Vonda Pestana
Editor: Angelique Campbell-Muir
Illustrations: Boris Silvestri and Melissa Webb
Reprint: Siew Han Ong

Acknowledgements
The author and publisher would like to acknowledge permission to reproduce material from the following sources:
AAP Image/AFP, p.25 top left; Amazon.com, p.27 bottom; Australian Picture Library/Corbis/Bettmann, pp.6 top, 16 top and bottom, 18 top and bottom /Schefler Collection, p. 6 bottom/Jim Richardson, p. 9 top /Jim Craigmyle, p. 9 bottom right /Laurent, p. 13/ Richard T.Nowitz, p. 14 top /Franken, p 14 bottom /John Garrett, p. 15/Museum of History and Industry, p. 17 bottom /Gunter Marx Photography, p. 26 bottom; Australian War memorial, p. 23; Digital Stock, p. 4 bottom left; Digital vision, p. 5 bottom; Newspix, p. 30 bottom; PhotoDisc, pp. 1, 8 top, 9 top and bottom left; PhotoEdit/Michael Neweman, pp. 12, 30 top; photolibrary.com/Index Stock, pp. 21 bottom left; PhotoEdit/Michael Newman, pp. 12, 30 top; photolibrary.com/Index Stock, pp. 21 bottom, 28-29 bottom / SuperStock, p. 22 bottom; Stock Photos /Masterfile/Ron Stroud, p. 5 top /John Felingersh, p. 7 bottom /Brian Sytnyk, p. 17 top; Stock Photos, p. 19 bottom left and right /Diana Calder, p. 8 left /Pauline Madden, p. 10 /John Oxley Library, pp. 12 inset, 26 top /RickAltman, o. 20.

PM Extras Non-Fiction
Ruby
Caring for the Earth
Changing Cultures
Having Fun, Then and Now
Change in the Community
Communities Everywhere
Past Work, Future Work

For product information and technology assistance,
in Australia call 1300 790 853;
in New Zealand call 0508 635 766

For permission to use material from this text or product,
please email **aust.permissions@cengage.com**

ISBN 978 0 17 011467 7
ISBN 978 0 17 011464 6 (set)

Cengage Learning Australia
Level 7, 80 Dorcas Street
South Melbourne, Victoria Australia 3205

Cengage Learning New Zealand
Unit 4B Rosedale Office Park
331 Rosedale Road, Albany, North Shore NZ 0632

For learning solutions, visit **cengage.com.au**

Printed in Australia by Ligare Pty Ltd
14 15 16 23 22 21

Contents

Chapter 1

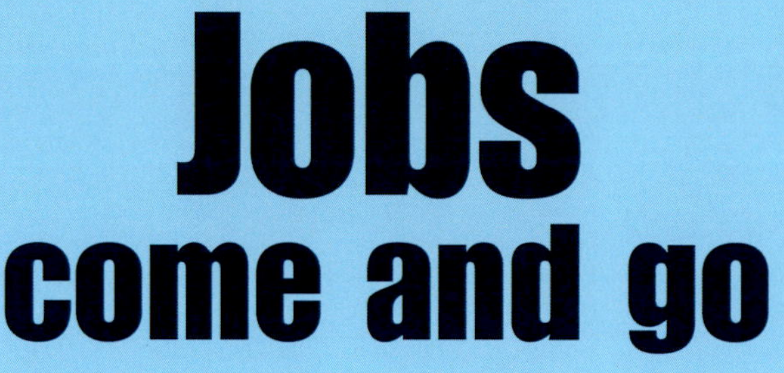

Jobs come and go

Hop in your time machine and travel back 20 years. When you get there, lean out the window and ask the first person you meet if they could help you find a web designer or a genetic engineer. Be ready for them to give you a blank stare.

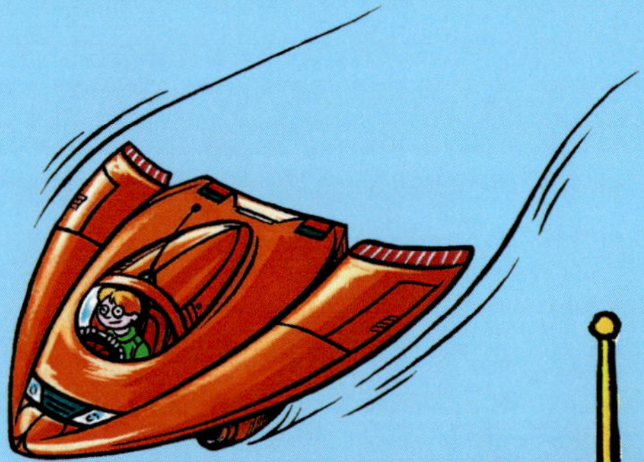

Go back another 30 years. Ask someone about working as an astronaut or a computer programmer. Odds are good they'll think you're weird.

Try a bigger jump. Set the dial for the year 1900. Ask someone about being a pilot, a car mechanic or a film director. More strange looks.

Jobs come. Jobs go. That's the way it has been for hundreds of years.

When no-one drives horse-drawn carriages, no-one needs a coachman. When everyone has a telephone, there's no need for telegram deliverers. And when someone invents a computer or a jet, we need people to build, fix, sell and operate them.

A few thousand years ago, choices were pretty limited – hunt, gather and do whatever was needed to survive.

But that's all different now. **Technology** constantly changes the way we live and the work we do.

Chapter 2

Why Work?

First, let's find out why people work.

Perhaps the answer seems obvious – you work to get money so you can buy things.

Imagine what it used to be like. You (or your family) made all your own clothes, grew your own food, made all your own tools, provided your own entertainment – the list goes on and on.

But not everyone was good at everything. Someone could shoe a horse, but did not like knitting. Or they could heal a wound, but could not tell a decent story.

So people divided up the work to take advantage of the different skills. Along the way, these activities turned into trades, businesses and jobs.

But don't people work for other reasons?

Work can make you feel useful or helpful. It's a way to contribute to the world. It can let you express yourself (whether you're an artist or a programmer). You can also meet people and learn new things.

Some people choose to work because they enjoy doing what they do.

Besides, what would it be like if no-one worked? Nothing would ever get done and people would get very bored.

Chapter 3

Life on the Farm

Until around 1700, people spent most of their working lives on two things – food and shelter. Work depended on muscle power more than brainpower. And if something needed to be made, it was usually made by hand (or maybe using a simple machine), by someone who lived nearby.

The idea of going to work for someone else to earn a wage had not been invented yet.

Most people simply farmed food or worked in a trade. Leading up to 1700, some manufacturing was done in homes. It was called **cottage industry**, and husband, wife and children all worked closely together.

A cottage industry today may or may not take place in a home, and may employ workers outside of the family.

Jobs of Old

People's work often became their last name. We still see these surnames today. Think about the origin of surnames like Baker and Tailor. What work do you think people with these names may have done many years ago?

Making candles the traditional way. This man i cutting the ends off these hand-dipped candles

Here are a few more examples:

A ...	Is someone who...
Cooper	makes barrels
Fletcher	makes arrows
Cartwright	makes wagons
Crocker	makes bowls (crockery)
Chandler	makes candles
Hatcher	raises chickens
Sawyer	saws (a carpenter)

A cooper making oak barrels.

Chapter 4

Work Revolution

Mine workers in 1908.

The **Industrial Revolution** changed everything. In the 1700s, people began to use steam-powered machines to make things. Machines meant work needed to be done in factories. This was faster and cheaper than cottage industries. Workers became more productive and no longer needed to be skilled in their craft. Prices dropped, so more people could afford to buy more things.

Before the Fair Labour Standards Act in 1938, many children worked the same hours as adults. This young girl is working in a cotton mill in North Carolina, USA.

At the same time, there were big changes in farming. The **Agricultural Revolution** saw better crop-growing, improved livestock breeding and new farm equipment. The result – more and more was produced by fewer and fewer people. Farms got bigger and often stopped growing food. Instead they turned to crops like cotton, which were needed as raw materials in **textile** factories.

So where did all the out-of-work farming families go? To the cities.

And where did they find work? In factories, mills and mines. Starting in the 1700s people moved to cities by the thousands.

Metal workers in a ship-building foundry around 1900.

Chapter 5

More Changes

The Industrial Revolution took both workers and work out of the home and moved them into the factory. Cities were busy, noisy, smelly and polluted. Many workers lived in cramped, dirty houses. They barely made enough money to survive. Men, women and even children all worked long hours in difficult, often dangerous, conditions.

Smokestacks in Pittsburgh, US in the 1890

Industrial Cities

Whole cities were built around single industries. Here are some examples:

Manchester, England,
had cotton and textiles

Pittsburgh, Pennsylvania, USA,
had steel

Glasgow, Scotland,
had shipbuilding

Where conditions were bad, workers began to demand improvement. Workers formed groups, called **unions**, so they could act together and bargain with employers and owners for more pay and safer working conditions. Often unions would go on **strike** to try to force an employer to meet their demands.

When workers go on strike, it can stop public transport systems or halt industry.

Chapter 

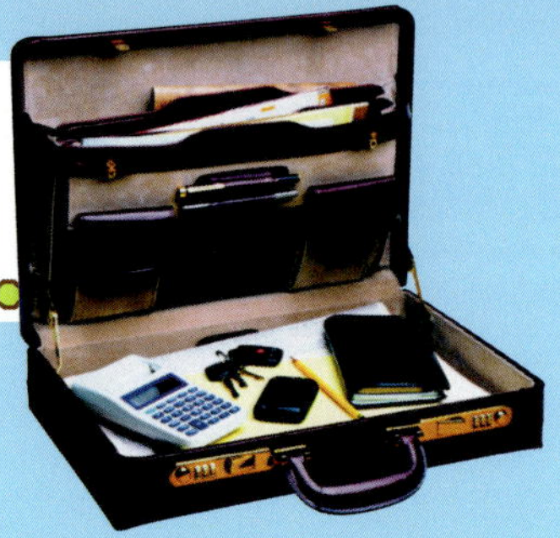

A Job for Life

Once the idea of a 'job' took hold, both employers and employees found that they liked stability.

Until only very recently, the late 1900s, many people spent their whole working lives with one business or one company. They learned a trade, such as welding or carpentry, then spent decades using what they'd learned.

In some places, a single industry, like mining or manufacturing, dominated a town. In these towns, grandfathers, fathers and sons often spent their whole lives working for one company.

The companies encouraged loyalty. Some provided housing and health care. Most contributed towards the workers' **pensions**. Often, there was a sense that the company would take care of you.

Workers punch into the time clock before they start work.

Chapter 7

Women and Work

By the early 1900s, the work that women did was very different from that of men. Men usually worked in manufacturing jobs and did professional work (like doctors and lawyers). Women mostly had clerical jobs (typing and filing), lower-paid factory positions, or worked as cleaners.

World War II changed all that. From 1939–45, as millions of men signed up to fight, there was a shortage of workers. Women stepped into jobs that only men had done, such as welding and building ships.

The world of work had changed forever. Women had become more confident. They enjoyed the independence, the money and the chance to learn new skills.

Chapter 8

Information Revolution

Just as women were taking on wartime jobs, the seeds for the next revolution were being planted. Electronic computers appeared during the war. Over the next half century, as they became smaller and more powerful, they quickly spread to every corner of modern life.

Computers sparked the Information Revolution. It changed how we store and access information, how we communicate and how we work.

If you wanted to draw the plans for the inside of a large building, it used to take a group of skilled draftsman two months to do the job. Software now means one person can do it in two days.

Chapter 9

The Amazing Disappearing Distance

In the 1800s, the railroad changed transportation. Never before had so many people travelled so far, so quickly and so often. The railway, more than any other means of transport before it (including ships), changed the way people thought about distance.

The Information Revolution is doing something similar today. But this time, distance is disappearing. Using a phone or a computer, you can reach anyone in the world, whenever you like. Cars can only transport us to limited places, but the internet can take us all around the globe.

'Electronic commerce', known as **e-commerce** or e-business, means doing business using the internet. This means that no matter how small your business, you can work from anywhere. Now your customers can be from around the world. In this way, many companies have become global businesses, meaning they deal with people all over the world.

Chapter 10

What will Work Life be Like?

By the time you start working, the world will again be very different. For one, a job for life is already a thing of the past. The odds of you working for only one or two companies during your life are almost zero.

More likely, you'll take a series of jobs or work in contract (temporary) positions to gain skills and experience.

You might work overseas for a while, and you might wait longer between jobs to get the right one. Plus, you'll probably have more than one career – a doctor might become a writer, then turn her hand to film making.

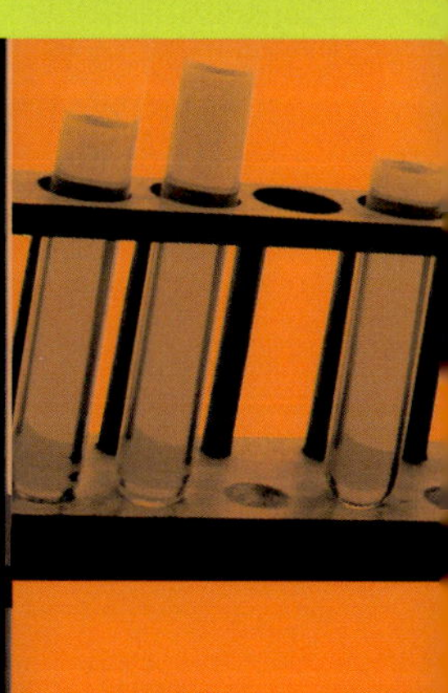

You might not find much full-time work either. Today more and more new jobs are part-time.

And your job may be something that hasn't been thought of yet. Sure, we'll still need jobs that are around now – chefs, mechanics, teachers, childcare workers and so on. But the Information Revolution has really only just started, so expect new jobs to keep springing up.

nd remember, you can lways start your own usiness and be the one ho creates jobs for ther people.

Glossary

Agricultural Revolution (also called Agrarian Revolution) a time during the 1700s and 1800s that saw major changes to farming practices, including more crops, better livestock breeding and new farm equipment

cottage industry a system of working and making things at home. Merchants provided the raw materials, the workers created the products, then merchants collected them and paid workers part of the price they received for selling the products. Common products were cloth and clothing

e-commerce short for electronic commerce, or business conducted electronically. Typically, this means using the internet to buy goods online, or using internet banking

Industrial Revolution a time during the 1700s and 1800s that saw the rise of mass-produced goods made by machines in factories

pensions money paid to workers upon retirement or disability

strike workers refusing to work to pressure their employer into meeting their demands

technology tools, knowledge and inventions that help people do things

textile a cloth or fabric

unions organisations of workers, usually from the same industry, dedicated to improving the working conditions faced by those workers.